'Happiness is being sure you're sure'
(Jack Cope)

'Only the gentle are ever really strong'
(James Dean)

To and Adrian with thanks

Testing the Edge

POEMS

MARK SWIFT

Mark 2003

SNAILPRESS

SNAILPRESS
30 Firfield Road, Plumstead 7800, South Africa

UK distribution:
With A Little Help, Providence House, 99 Mawson Road,
Cambridge CB1 2DZ, England

Poems in this collection have appeared in the following
publications:
In South Africa: *Contrast, UpStream, New Contrast, New Coin, The
Paperbook of South African English Poetry* (Ad Donker, 1986),
Broken Strings, The Politics of Poetry in South Africa (Maskew
Miller, 1992), *The Heart in Exile, South African Poetry in English,
1990-1995* (Penguin, 1995) and *Carapace.*
In the UK: *Envoi, The Rialto, Agenda, Iron, Orbis* and *The Frogmore
Papers.*

'Canvas and Ashes' won the Thomas Pringle Poetry Prize
(1987).

© Mark Swift 1996
First published 1996
ISBN 1-874923-34-5

Back cover photograph by Adam Swift
Cover illustration by Mark Swift
Typeset by User Friendly
Printed and bound by Interpak

For
Adam and Dylan
(my sons)

Andrew and Lila
(my godchildren)

M A R K   S W I F T was born in Queenstown, South Africa, to a family with a British 1820 Settler history. He was educated in Cathcart, Cape Town and East London. After completing art studies, he worked as a journalist on the *Cape Times* and *The Argus*. Now in England, he is employed by the *Cambridge Evening News*.

His poems, prose and criticism have been widely published in newspapers and leading literary magazines in South Africa and in the UK and in numerous anthologies. His first collection of poems, *Treading Water*, won the Ingrid Jonker Prize for the best debut volume in Southern Africa and was distributed in the UK by Carcanet. His second book, *Gentlewoman*, had a history of banning and unbanning in South Africa. It ran to two editions and was also published by Grosset & Dunlap in New York. A third volume, *Seconds Out*, appeared in 1983. In 1987 he was awarded the Thomas Pringle Prize for poetry by the English Academy of Southern Africa. Swift's poems have been broadcast by the BBC, the SABC and Canadian radio.

He is divorced and has two sons, Adam and Dylan.

Also by Mark Swift:
Treading Water, David Philip
Gentlewoman, Don Nelson
Seconds Out, Bateleur Press

CONTENTS

ON THE ROAD

Under a big sky the oil-reeking car
smokes on through the miles,
    plunging down lanes
on stone-old farms in search
of pasture and place. Moons
    and suns collide on the eye,
        blazing our vagrants' trail.

In a race of cloud over hard-bitten
earth, birds are fired
    from the bow of instinct; arrowing
home to Africa. Sleeping on the wing,
slit-eyed over dreaming ships,
    they hitch a ride
        on the full-fledged wind.

Instinct goads our own wild trek
from the stones of runic
    mountains. This is travel
by numbers; or by pins thrust
into maps. On strange roads, under
    footloose stars, we home in
        on exile.

TALKING IN MY SLEEP

(Cambridge '87)

This was the year of days,
of wild hallucinations
in the gravel pit; it was a bier
   rotting in a roofless church, a Welshman
    mad through the glass
      of a car.

     And my country burning
in the cyclops eye. I was all nations,
all bewildered provinces; lost in a tearabout
   of motorways.

At this remove – somewhere
in an Atlas – the African dead
fall clearly to mind. Those bundles
   of clothing; the awkward sleepers
   on township streets.

Birds are the only freedom; the beasts
are all for burning. The feathered exiles
come and go, raucous in dialect, flouting
   the seas on a wing and our prayers.

If the world does turn
my dreams will leave me standing. I cannot
risk a flat-earth bed; the awkward
   dead never cease
     walking in my sleep.

CANVAS AND ASHES

(For Enslin du Plessis)

        Old man,
you died too late to live, for grief
    to nag at your memory. Crawling veins
in your leafy palms betrayed
            blue winter, the ache of frost in
                branches of bone. Fingers gnarled
    on pens toiled open
            in the dark, reached for the nipple, caressed
                remembered thighs
            as love dreamt a man
who slept entire as a child.

        Death takes the best
                and the worst – your mind hitched
a ride to gentle stars; on the Styx the killers
                screamed under sail as black water
    thundered. Skulls were split to the tooth, lawyers
    and lenders tore coins from your eyes.

        On veld near the tides we see you still, your
    churchill-bulk under straw hat; the pens
                and brushes at feeble play. No fire there
to set the world alight; all thumbs, your addled canvas
            was women away from youth's deft
hand; the sweep of charcoal and passion.

        In African dusk you share cheap pine
    with my loved and lost – a sepia
                nurse, kilted men; my burning son with
        rapt eyes fixed
on your shutter-foxed head. You left no saddled horse, no
                dangling wife or son in cast-off
    black. The London streets are a shadow
            short; no other shadows mourn.

11

TESTING THE EDGE

(For Justin Brooks, 1969-1995)

Out on the wire there's margin
for error, the bow-strung
   man is feathered
for flight. In the glare of light
resurrection is plain,
      Icarus rises,
         night after day.

Out on the wire the music
begins. The walker, sleep-dancing,
   perplexes his limbs,
conjuring up the broken wings
      on sawdust.

It's the waltz of death, this airy
glide to a self-defeating end.
      The perilous few who saunter
to the limit are poised
      yet again
on a filament wired
      to the moon.

A crisis of nerve on time's
trapeze invites their swift
   descent; down at wing, the faltering
      birdmen plummet.
The darkened earth, as wide
   as a grave, makes light
      of their fall from grace.

FRONTIER FIRES (1820-1984)

(A trilogy)

I

On foot-pad streets
the moon announces
    cold steel; blades
      quicken
in their bodies' dark sheaths.
This avid kindling; dry bone
    and threadbare flesh,
  flares
    in the moment's heat.

II

Rawhide and wax,
elbow-greased wood, connived with flame
  to steal a march
    on the dawn. Herds in the dust
  and ham-strung flocks
    went down to the drovers'
knives. The earth was on its rounds,
    time on its beat
and makers were lost
to their world. What lends substance
  to those pale men
    is history put to the torch.
  Their gutter-tongues
put noun to valley
  and headstone; rough vowels
    were sown as seed. These ancient
  names survive
the brutal christening; a baptism
    by fire.

III

The scorched earth
of Africa burns; a pall blears over
the city. Birds toil
in thermals, the sun
staggers dazed
to the cooler west.
After the fires, the blown ashes
on windy veld
loosely define the stolid chair, pioneer's
Bible; the creaking ligaments
of a leather-strung bed.
Under the moon – by implication –
the charred world
is immaculate.

IN MEMORIAM

(For friends in South Africa)

Hemingway said
never count your
casualties
gentlemen.

KIA is OK
But what about
the
Walking Wounded?

HOME THOUGHTS

(For Sarah and Paul)

There is no road home
        for home is where the heart is.
                We are
                voyagers, we carry
our journeys within us. Privateers,
        we run before a fickle wind.
        Each day defines a course; its fixed
                imperative. Out on the jet
streams, adrift for days, we navigate
        the tide-bound globe. We are all
        Columbus, quaffing
sour water under creaking stars
                till moonfall.

        I fly, as unerring
as a bird, between two departures.
                One lies
dark, skeletal; the other is verdant,
        a wildness of birds and gunfire.
                With renegades
        from every corner of the shrinking
world, I discuss, duty-free,
                the love of distant friends,
        the lure of the sun
and the arid wines of another place. We share
                the east, the south; go west
        before closing time.
Far above, on migratory trails,
                the gypsies at heart
                fly home and away.

IN THE ROMAN ARENA

(Saintes, France)

In the barren arena the stones
   are still, the careful mortar
     is dead to the touch. We cock an ear
regardless, alive to the notion
        of fear and applause
   driven deep to the core
     of this white
blind place. Every arch, every broken
   frieze, is a headstone and an epitaph.

These weathered remains attest to
   their brutal cause; to men on their
     march to bewildered ends
of unwanted earth. No bones come
        to light, no hanks
   of hair; the legions of Rome
        are dead to the world.

A slow, hot wind unfolds over
   granite; trifles with the words
     of the living. No murmurs of the past
intrude. The dead men, the shakers of
        the earth, hold no sway
   in their dust. The mouths of their
        victims, swordsmen
and beast, are wide in a rictus
   of silence.

Only the wind and water endure. Above
   the chiselled strata, cupped in
     stone, dark water wells
from its pagan shrine. Sullen, shiftless,
        it bleeds forever
   from a wound that will not heal.

The short-lived birds,
as raucous as mortals, tell the hour
through swings of their pendulum.

THE LAST LION

Long in the tooth
the killer of lions sat glaucous-
eyed in his hide-strung chair. Burned
to the bone, his skin was eroded
by wildlife trails
on the watering-hole
of his face. In his rough-baked
house the sun etched its
shadows of thorn. His trophies
bared their rib-breaking fangs: the leopard,
the cheetah, the Last Lion
in his pride of place. Now, no grief attaches
to the dusty, worm-riddled head. The hunter,
with his great, cuffing paws, his low-slung
gait and vacant snarl, was
the last of the beasts. Holed up
on his hill, caged by empty
spaces, he talked of the ambush; the oiled
snick of a worn bolt, the howl triggered
deep in a heart-stopped throat. Stalked
by every dawn, cornered
in the dark with his shaggy mane
and blunted eyes, he was prey
to the one unerring assassin; time
with its claws unsheathed
for the kill.

STAG AT BAY

(For my grandfather)

Bamboo-backed, my Bengal Lancer
    (long-dead)
colonises rooms forever. Sam-Browned, pithed
and polished, he gazes out with bland
    illogic from a sepia world.
Behind him, in parentheses, is a tower
      of Sikh; lush mouth
      dictating a beard.

His was a tale of uneasy truce
      over India and old Kaffraria, indexed
        now in a regiment's tome. In the absence
    of battle, his warring peace, love
inflicted its wounds. His first wild
wife, a frontier girl, danced naked
      under moons; died with the day
and the birth of her child.

    The second,
perilous-eyed, lay mooning in the sun,
    mistress of all she deigned
    to survey. A cuckold, now, he left
my mother to the love of God
    and forgiving aunts.

The years pounded by like scouts in pursuit,
    running down the past, kicking up dust; obscuring
      his grief in some distant grave.
And now his beauty, his fickle betrayer, is tucked
    into earth; an aged,
      wrinkled child.

Perhaps, in rearguard surrender, he sees
    grey hair as a dark tumble
        of leaves on the stone
of her pillow; reaches out for her map
        of skin, traces the route
from cheekbone to lip
        that was journeyed before
by a singular man – his only hated
            enemy.

MEADOWS OF THORN

The fixed, knee-high
        boys
take in baked space, the man
        stalking – three across,
four down – the confines
    of his mind. The eyes
        of harder fathers
            closed
on the same coarse hills; their bones
    obsess the farm.

    Stockyards and dreamers
throw shadows on sand; night
    takes them all to task. The sower
scrawls his hieroglyphs
        in a ledger
        of debit and loss; sheep gag
    on his meadows of thorn.

    Within the barbs
of his boundary, nailed to the sky,
    a mute, crossed Christ
        in a rusted suit
            scares crows and
    the children away. Doors
to their granite rooms are closed
            on farmyards
    of broken tin cows.

    At home as the hills,
with deft hands
    on stoic clay, the black youths
            conjure
        their furious bulls.

ALL AT SEA

(For Peter, Emma and Nicholas)

The hundred voices
    of a wooden ship
murmur on the creaking tide.
    Only a man and the moon
are still. Adrift on the night,
    he gazes out from the crow's
    nest of his land-lubber's head.

    All the seas
of the drowning world nudge
    and shove at the derelict shore; the sky
    swings at anchor. Street-wise,
sea-foolish, the man
    persuades a candle to cast
    thin light on his shadow.

Above him, the stars
    steer a course to empty
reaches where the compass locks
    on a grave-point. Below, the sharks
    muscle in on his waking dreams.

    All frail boats
are dowelled and clinkered
    sailors; all earthbound men are
tooled and shaped for the waves. The man
    sounds his depths, the sea plumbs
    his shallows. Tide
        after tide, his pen goes
    to paper; the strangest
    voyage begins.

SHADOWS ON THE WALL

(For my mother)

Under the toiling tree-tops, always
   in a high wind, my aunt's house
     sagged under dripping
  eaves. Window-warped,
     barred to the light, it kept
       her darker secrets. Beneath
the hunchbacked sofa, behind the laden
   sideboard, the past was put
     to rights; never swept away.

Outside, a living, sprung and tender
   world lay breathing and open.
     On green mornings, berry-mad,
  we scratched like chickens
     in the undergrowth. Hot on the
       warpath, armed to the teeth,
we stalked our childhoods till bedtime.

Adrift on feathers, creaking through
   the long nights, I followed the moon
     as it tugged at its tides
  for no reason or rhyme. In her
     sanctum, her spinstered room
       with its china and lace,
a lover gloomed down out of tarnish.
   Her dresses, wallflowers
     in a wardrobe, had ceased their dance.

Alone in her brown study, she pinched
   her pennies, counted her griefs
     as blessings coined
  by a thriftless God. The telephone
     slept on its cradle, no visitors
       called, and death when it came
     did not knock.

Sunday birds

In the church ringed by surpliced
trees, voices soar in spires
        of sound. The dumb-struck stones are still,
clouds walk on water.
    All the streets are bright streams; the wings
of shadows feather on walls
        of burnt brick.
    The birds are deaf to the ranting
priest; from altars of the wind they scan
the buttressed earth, the fount of holy, salty sea.

Feeling his wings, his fine feathers
        of gold and lace, the priest cajoles
his earth-bound flock. These, the landlords of spirit,
        will soon be tenants of silent soil.

The birds are careless in prayer; they praise
the world with rapture. On the tower
        of the bell, on leafy pews, wicked starlings
        are talking in tongues.

BENEATH THE TOR

(In Gorse Cottage, Dartmoor)

Sky-high on a wind-whip
of moor my wife was teaching the
boy to read. Through the papered walls
of a quarryman's house his halting
lilt (her bridle-tug
of tongue) voiced
his stumble
toward a literate deceit.

Curled on a bed too wide (I can sleep
only to ruins, now, or an image
of Christ) I conjured up
the giant Tor; the bloodied
rock on the moor. Leaved in lava, it is
hewn on pages of silence.

A place of tears,
of sacrifice, it cannot sleep or
speak. Fused to the bones of the
basalt sky, its tongue is locked
on confession.

I dreamed
of Roundheads, rusted to the
eyes; of blood and iron on the wild,
clenched hill. I awoke
to incantations, to the wind
rubbing at the words
of the child, a shout away
from the unread rock, the dumbfound
tablet of runic stone
calling soldiers
and boys up to die.

GREEN WARRIOR

Through sun-shocked glass
the tree towered clean; a green
warrior
rooted to the spot
by chance. Seething
with flocks
and cornered gales, its hissed
commands, imprecations, entered
my bedroom window.

Today the axeman throws
his weight, the air
vibrates to a throaty
saw's catarrh. The great
bent shield gives up
the ghost of its shadow.

The street is a winding-
sheet: all things – birds
and the gales, trees and
mountain – toil towards ruin. Time
hefts a sun-bright
blade; felling its forests of men.

.

NIGHT MOVES

Wrapped in a shroud, a spread-eagled
    man lies dreamless
    in the unmade grave of his bed.
In the dead of dark, footpad
    shapes mutter and scratch
    in the rafters. A tooth is bared
on his mooning face, his hand is clenched
        on the night's long throat.

Worlds away, a breath apart, a woman
    hates in her eyes. Closed to touch, she
    shudders to sense the predator
in his cage barred by bone. A bird
    cajoles the dawn; flat stars
    primp in water. A clock toils on.

These are the strangers; the victors
    in defeat. In wars of the board, white
    knight to reckless queen, she was woman
made of flowers. Now she burns
    in her autumn; the man lies dazed
    in her leaves. They are checked
    and mated, wedded
        to their game.

The woman is alone; she is rib and withered
    Eve. Destiny scrabbles
    in the rafters, the man sleeps
on. Her clock continues
    its countdown; her petals clamber
     softly to the floor.

SALVAGE OF THE SAILOR AND THE POET

(For Caroline and Jamie)

In the grip of dusk
the sea tears paper; scribbles the moon
　　　on pages of sand. A screeching sailor
　　gulls under clouds, hauling his feathers
to compass-points
　　　of the tide-tossed dead. His eyes
　　are hawsered to wrecks of men, to white bone
and canvas wings,
　　　beating
　　beating, on the cabined roof
　　　　of the sinking sea.

Beached by windlassed tides, you, vivid
woman, cast a shadow-huge cross. Waves and
　　　your child
　　　　inform the world
　　that movement
　　is all there is. Eternity flames
in the sailor's wings; burns in the limbs
　　of the boy walking – on and in the water.

Green sea and breakers of dune
connive with the knock-kneed Canute: your son
　　　winching the sea back
　　with a tidal shout of joy; cupping the holy
　　　　water
　　in a tiny chalice of hands.

At his command the waves part,
tear a strip off the funeral sands; the drowned man
　　　in the live bird
　　wings salvaged into grace. From the deep-sea
grave of my plundered ship
　　I walk the plank; I scramble
　　　　to life
　　on a pirated rigging of air.

27

EXILE ON HIGH STREET

Out on a limb, the makeshift man,
I wax as the day wanes;
haunting the dead down
    canyon streets in the
        grave-robber dusk.

Stranger, stranger, stretch out
your hand; I shall bite it
off at the wrist. (Clouds flag in
tatters from the telephone
    wires, their empty sleeves
        are biceped by the wind.)

Stranger, stranger, give me
your wife; I shall tattoo her
with the needle-point of my
desire. (The birds are smuts in the
    chimney draughts, their wings are
        leather and ice.)

Stranger, stranger, give me
your house; I shall topple its
rooftree, scatter its stones. (The wafered
moon is drawn and quartered, smeared
    in haste on a blackboard.)

Stranger, stranger, give me
your land; I shall sow its fields
with twisted roots. (The giant oak has
a mildewed heart, its branches are rotted
    to the sky.)

Stranger, strangers, I give you
my death: Like the sun, I leave barefoot
prints on your hobnailed floors, naked
space where my flesh stalked. The shadow
of my shadow falls –
on a world that is all
your own.

WHAT'S IN A NAME

*(There are the graves of some soldiers ... and the remains of
Fort Michel. It has become Fort Mitchell, but was named after
Colonel Michel of the Warwickshire Regiment – 'Guide to the
Hogsback'.)*

Down in the baking Tyumie
Michel's reluctant Horse dragged spoor
for the wild men of the valleys.
On the Hogsback now the settlers talk
of hydrangeas. It's Mitchell's
Fort and pass, and impis
of quavering, insistent boys on the tar
sell horses tailed with mane. Painted, cold
clay, they break a leg
down the blood-red slope where Michel cajoled
his unfired troops. Conjecture
remarks on his few remains,
the absence of bullet and button; the havoc
played with his name.
When heat translates the air to rain
the trees lose substance, thorn connives
with Japanese oak. Break
a leg, cry the birds from their fortified crags;
break a name.

LAND WARS

(For Anthony Bartlett, 1948-1995)

Lost together, close in a growling
of mastiffs, we stalked
the perimeter. Behind
and beyond
the wire, the puffadders lay
beneath paintings on rock,
their jaws unhinged
among bones and shards.

Hammering up the mountain
we crushed wild geraniums,
startled stock untamed
on their barren slopes.
Below us, in Goshen, the youths
could hear the rumble,
the thunder, of men in search
of a higher gear; a better view.

Guns come easy
to the shoulder. Through
a scope
I scanned the horizon; drew
a bead on emptiness. At the fire,
with the dark closing in, I
staked my claim on fear.
The wire kept the world out,
it kept us within.
We were lords of nothing
our eyes could survey.

DREAMS OF THE GRASS

Where crows slang on their pulpit
    of rocks a virgin dreamed
        a husband
up from her loosened thighs.
Fumble-thumbed, he yearned in his tousle
    of grass; a cautious Adam
        till their feral caress
in the vivid dark of her ambush.

Wise to change, as still as
    the past, she awakes each day
        to her dream. Her children
chaver on bird-light limbs. They are
wild in the trees, as flushed
    in their sleep as apples.

The man is a brother to
    the wind. He speaks, and ice
        breaks. He wears down the years
with his restless heels, lovers'
breasts are shaped in his hands.

The woman withers in her fecund
    spring. Leaves drift
        from the evergreens; water
is dead to its roots. The man
fumbles at buttons for words, she draws
    blood from her tongue.

All her children have gone
    to crusades, trudging down on small
        red feet
to the empty sea. They are fishes
and tiny loaves; grist for the mill
    of the world. The boys are tousled
        in long grass, the girls lie
dreaming; their hands in prayer
    between closed thighs.

MAKING A POINT

*(For Gus. Based on the assumption that experience
interrogated is not the experience.)*

The poem is a line
scrawled in such a manner
that it is no longer
the shortest distance between
two points

(Dotting the i's and crossing
the t's is an experience
in itself)

FLOWER GIRL

I dial your number in
the depths of sleep; no throaty voice
replies. Hands on the clock
move; hands on my body move.
There is a flower in your
mouth, there are flowers
in your thighs. Alone,
sleepless in the English dark,
I ache for doubt.

Always, in the garden
of you, is the flower
of your mind. Others
bend to privilege; they pluck at
your petals, consign them
to the wind – she loves me,
she loves me not.
She loves; she loves me not.

WINDVOGEL MOUNTAIN

(Cathcart, Eastern Cape)

From this fastness, this haphazard
        castle of stone and air, we straddle
            the galleries daubed by San.
Below us, on painted rock, the long-dreamed,
        long-dead kudu are brought to their knees
                by pin-pricks.

Hills away, a slow-coach train draws
        a thin, black line
            across ochre impasto. The centipede
of iron and its distant halt, a half-baked
        town on the rim of the world, betray
                the advance of history, of hair-trigger men
                    on the make.

This is the landscape of the brutal mind,
        beyond the reach of compass
            or intention. It is cradle
and deathbed, slung between poles of dawn
        and darkness, of fire and ice.

Below us, in their warrens, the hunters cowered
        as quarry, driven to earth by shod
            and blinkered centaurs. Men of the sky,
at home on the wind, they were brought to their knees
                with their painted prey.

LANDFALLS

(For Dylan, Rose Street, Edinburgh)

On the beach, high
and unhinged, I await
the Sesame; the door creaking open
to Paddy's bar. All night, yawing
through Scotland on the top
deck of a coach at sea (pitching
and heaving through grass-green swells)
I thought of you. Small son, charting
your course over Doldrums
of carpet or sleep. Landfalls
and legends are nothing to your
brave voyage; pressganged on towpath
walks over landlocked fens.
With my eyes turned in on a warm,
southern sea I offer no haven, no safe
anchorage. Still, we make
a separate peace. With winter
here and the ducks gone we will feed
the river together; cast our bread
on flat water
toiling to be waves.

AFTER THE READING

After the poems
the creaking stanzas of a bed
    versed in love. Skinned from a woman,
a jersey-pelt lay warm on the floor.

And all the leaves
    were named. The tree through glass
was a tree through glass
with its roots thrust deep
    into syllables.

Nothing was new
    under sun or moon; limping endearments,
our clumsy asides, had twisted the tongues
of dumbstruck lovers
    now in the clutch of the earth.

After the reading
we lapsed into mute acceptance. Our eyes
    spoke volumes. Sibilant
ribbons, our rivers of breath, wound
their way to a separate sleep; to dark oceans
    of infinite silence, lapping at the bed
        and the grave.

CAMBRIDGE BLOU

The wind blows cold
        down Norfolk Street, stirring up
the detritus; the cartons and the fag-ends.
    My maligning eye takes in
            the rotten row, the houses
out at elbows in the care-worn
            dusk.

    Beyond the bridge
            and a sodden Green the ham-strung
Cam chews its cud. In the frigid dawn
    I fill empty hands with bones
            from a glove; death burns in each
            cigarette.

    Under lowering skies the great
            stones of the city settle; a chapel
spire draws a bead on God. In chavering
    trees the birds of the world
            select delegates to parley.

    Here, the bitter, yellow
            wind stirs paper in lieu of leaves;
a blind man, his hands outstretched,
    takes his sighted stick for a walk.

    In the pinched gardens Roman shards
            and trivial bones come to light
with the thrust of a spade; grave is heaped
    on forgotten grave. Under vaults
            in the chapels the chiselled
giants are as cold as stone in their sculpted
    folds. No pupil informs their granite
            eyes; they are deaf
    to the judgement of mortals.

The blind man is in better shape. A heap
　　　　　of clothes on scuffed shoes,
he taps his relentless morse; a code
　　of passage from his world's end
　　　　　　　to his bed on the unmade graves.
The Romans are bones, the giants are dead,
　　the old man sees
　　　　　　through the void.

HOLY MOTHER

Mother of all that is holy
make lambs of us all. From
the ram take the crumpled
horn. From the ewe take the pouch
of blood. From the sheath
of the man
take the sword. From the sheath
of the woman take the man.
Holy Mother
with love that endureth
make holy fools of us all.

Tongues of Stone

The words of the Welsh
are stones in water, pebble-smooth
and rounded. From a granite house
   on a smoking hill
   I tongue my African gutturals; a far
hawk's cry from the throaty vowels
      of these lucid streams.

   This, too, is a place of
skulls, of green jaws and helmets
of bone. The dreams of princes
   harp in their ruins; their renegade
   horses go stamping by
      in the unsaddled dark.

   On the shiftless, tilting hills, foxes
slake their urgent thirst
on hot blood, buzzards on the wings
   of a ragged wind drag shadows
   of panic over carrion fields.

   Still, these are only the windfalls
of death: a breeze pummels a tree; fruit
falls. Here, the ambush of history
   is over; the ink has dried
   on paper and leaves.

   In the stone house
on a slide of green (not a sheep
out of place) the unruly Welsh see me
   slant through a glass. With a shift
   of dusk and inflection
their meadow becomes my place
      of skulls; a boneyard
of veld. Wordless, I hear voices garbled
      in water. A hawk tears eyes

from living lambs, the children
shriek at their deadly play. I cup hands
   to the ears
      of my helmet of bone.

NEST OF THE EAGLES

(For Sue and Gabriella)

To paint the hill in a poem
   I write your windows
      framing poplars; laughter
among pines, a bird on
      thinnest air. To paint a poem
on the hill I stroke
the urgent growth of your hair, shock
      to your mouth, let the rivers
run through your wrists.

To paint you on the hill
   I abandon paper for the quick
      of the tongue. Words as wild
as darkness marry
      root to branch, granite
to the sky. We are
the poem, we are images couched
      in language and ferns. We are
figures drawn on a landscape, daubed
   by the sun. We are painted
      lovers on the painted hill.

BACKTRACKS

(For my brothers)

We will not go
that way again. Where the
houses ended and the world began
childhood's trail runs cold.
From high blue dawns to the smother
of night we shrieked in our game.
Barebacked riders, wild
on wheels, we were deaf to whispers
of downfall. We do not recall
departure; grudging out
from that tin-pot,
canting town,
perched on the edge of our father's grave.
Smoke in the wind was reason enough
to blear at our eyes
with roughened hands.

Lives later
we clamoured by
in a roil of dust, tearing past the old house,
our bivouac of granite
with its tree-top yacht
and jungle shrubs; its wild oceans
of lawn. Without us,
the town still chafes in its rough,
African night. Teeth clash
in a whinny of words
over tepid gin, a mile short of the windscape
and fear, with its picked white bones and
painted caves. The moon
still rides roughshod over rooms
where we slept in the trusting dark
while jackals tore
the throats from lambs

Baby talk

For the new-born child
the night bears a thumb-print,
        the smudged impression
    of a hand
    that leaves the sky ajar.
            All conception
        is immaculate: the last of the salt
            on new-baked bread.
    In his swaddle of flesh the child hears
    the ancients grouse; the old made
            new in our gabbles of love.
    In a dead-end lurch
from cradle to grave and back
        again we pray
            for the faith to conceive
        of prayer. Cut down
    to size, we chapel our palms,
            voice old pleas
        to quicken our dead. Belief shifts
            to a feasible focus, to the fearful
comfort of the strangers with whom
        we shape old clay. With a heft of hands
    the child shifts
            to a doting hip. We murmur
our language of God. Hatred. Fear.
            Deceit. The door to wonder
                swings closed.

At this time

Here, now, at this time
        I grieve
for friends who have died.
        There is nest, there is sky –
the scanty tree
wears its hard-won green
        for a while.

Second string

A horse
Too brutally bred
I have weak knees
        A hardened jaw
Some fatal flaw

ASHES IN THE MOUTH

The cold, hard voices
of the birds tell of order, of chaos behind
our shutters of lace. With a
foot in the grave, another on
the passage to a bottle of wine
and its ruin of a friend,
the tears runnel down.

Fathers and lovers are clenched
in the earth, beyond the reach
of birdsong and prayer. Time is counted
sip by sip; our sands run
through the glass.

With the dregs drained, the friend
in his ruin, I plead with my dead
to set the clock an hour
before or after. It becomes
a sad pursuit, this arrival
at departure; the long sleep-walk
to a measured end. Always,
out of the blue, it is closing
time. All too soon,
last orders.

PILGRIMS' PATH

(Dordogne, France)

At Rocamadour the sword
   of myth is clenched in stone.
      On the reeling cliffs the tourists
swill red wine and plot
   their raids. The bells clang out
     below on the tortured
       pilgrims' road.

Mortared to rock, the floor of
   the ancient church is smoothed
     by the guilt of kings on their knees.
The Black Virgin has loosened
   thighs; her basalt face
   is cunning in prayer.

Envoys with no brief, travellers make
   their fleeting obeisance
     to place. Avid, unseeing, their eyes
are lenses intent on an image
       already consigned to the past.

Away from the tumult, a woman
   prays in her creases
     of fabric and flesh. Her yearning
Christ, betrayed each day, slumps
   in his hangnail of wounds. Up the fossiled
     steps, footsore, a son labours with a chair
       on wheels; up through the stations
     of his father's cross.

AT NOON

The San
made the buck
happen
in their eyes

The Xhosa
make the cow
happen
in their eyes

The Zulu
make the earth
happen
in their eyes

The white man
wears dark glasses
He makes
night and the wind
happen

Touch down

(Airport hotel, Gatwick)

Slick from the shower
barefoot
on the marble
(probably not)
of my bathroom
I hear
the dragon-
breathing
of the jets
in their compound
thrusting
to reverse
all forces
including those
of home

They promise the earth
these mules
old plodders of the air-
space
with their touch-
me-downs
from Bangkok
to Libreville
and
(just occasionally)
destinations
that matter
more
than the journey.

WINGS ON THE DARK

We go swiftly; clods shrapnel
   our last narrow cell and brass
     is dulled in a grief
       of earth. Our household
  trash, our treasures, are scavenged
again. Elbows grease our tables; chairs
    protest as the weight of the living
  descends. We go swiftly.

We go in silence, deaf to the thud
    and smother of soil. Our few tired
     loves, our triumphs
  over their reason, take steps
to recall the frightened heart, the erosion
  of tears on a face brow-beaten
    by time.

They dream of our dreams; they awake
  alone. Our dumb-found words
    are scrawled in the margins
of rooms; our silence is complete.
    High above the toiling
  waves they see burnt scraps
    of paper; a scribble of birds
     on the tide-washed
  slate of the sky. Out of the blue
a hawk stoops – and even those ashes
    are gone.

WALKING WOUNDED

In the bars of Marans
the calloused men leave sweat
on their fondled money. The great
lorries – intent on distance – thunder by,
shaking the thin, drab street
with its hanging gardens
of laundry. Only the agile brush, the rules
of thumb, lend charm to the torpid town.
The orange slant of tiled roofs, the quirks
of alleys, lend themselves to framed
perspective. Not the short-changed men or the washed
out, sudsy women,
stitched into aprons.
All wars are won, all battles
are lost; the carnal flowers are fed
by the graves of sons and fathers
in their hectic prime. In the shuttered gloom
faces are broken by light
and by time; a scowling youth
yearns out at the street with
exile and freedom in mind. On the windy
square the dead strike a pose; their startled
heroics are bloodless in stone. Only
the women are wounded. All their eyes
are sad farewells. It takes no art
to see dimension in these
still lives, these knotted sisters;
luminous in their mourning.

IN BERNIE'S GARAGE

(Cape Town, '92)

Whaddya doin, Pete? Looning
    around in Bernie's
garage, dead
drunk among lures, minnows,
    varnished rods and traces; old
huckleberry, propped up on two fours
by oil-slicked jeans (they could boogie by
    themselves and probably do).

Whaddya doin, my mate? Sliding in
and out of rage and joy at the shock
    of me, jaded from flight. Big
fish – you think – wrenched from
the air to be landed gasping on your
    bleak rock; my skin changing
colour, my eyes glazing over
at the bite – the hook – of your sour
    Cape wine.

All pretence is gone now, cast aside.
    You drink to be sober. You haunt
the wilder shore; sane-alone
    in your madness. Behind you,
    twice, I saw your death in the
fishermen's clutter – the nets
and gaffs, the hooks barbed for the
    big ones; the dreams that get away.

    Your eyes went out
to the sky at dawn, to the thunder
    of early surf. Out there, somewhere
    at the end of the line, is your great,
improbable kill: the blooding of your guilt.
    You know how you're doing, Pete
    – better than I.

49

DOWN TO THE WIRE

(At Charlie's. For Oona)

We burned in the slow
   heat of a summer
   turned sunny side up
but sombre with misgivings.
    Stilting girl, as strange
    as fact, you made fiction
of my fears; lies of
   the comforting truths.

On the billows of your bed
      we made
   love like a tide, tossed
   high and dry on a dune
     of sheets
when the last wave broke.
    No-one drowned; we dreamed instead.
    We clutched at straws and
    survived each other.

No tides batter here, there is
   only the flat, watery waste
   of damp fen wrested
     from the inland sea.
     Horizons shrank
in the undersea, upstairs room. We explored
   the known indefinite; found ciphers
   to unspoken codes.

There was you. There was me. The
   telephone played its numbers
     game; totting up short-
   circuits of loud and static
     anger. We went down to the
   wire, subtracted but not
    diminished. I still rise as a

Lazarus, up from our sheets, those
shrouds of fear and
                silence. Together, we kill to resurrect;
                day after winter's day.

SHADOW WORLD

                Through glazed glass
and a high, flocked sky, the sunless
days crowd in; the leaves of a calendar
                scurry in the back-biting, Siberian
                eddies of these blackland fens. In a
                        damp and papered grave
                for the living, the voices of the
tongue-tied, the sleep-awake,
are sweated into
                        impoverished brick
                        and the dumb crannies
                of the roof-space.

                Under a bigger sky my shadow
was thrown onto rockface and hard-baked
                veld. Cast by the moon, it was dragged
by tides over prow-beaten swells.
                Here, in the soft green, I am torn
                        for days from that rumpled
fugitive dogging my heels. Under different,
                        indifferent stars
I awake in dread of the exile's
                end, the foreign room or corner
                where that shadow will run me
                        down and into the ground. I erode
                the pavement from early dark
                   to the frigid dawn;
                        walking over my grave.

STICKS AND STONES

(Two poems)

I

Out of the frying
pan out of the fire
　　　we feel no chill. Ashes
sift down; we warm
　　　to the shapes
　　　　　　of strangers.
　　　We are flint
without spark; cold stone.
　　　I love you
we whisper to silence. We mouth
the words out of silence.

I am dragged from sheets
　　　to mirror
　　　the night's corrosion;
lines eating deeper,
　　　the worried brow
　　　　　　in retreat.
　　　I say, I whisper
why break my bones, why
　　　　　　murder with words.

II

On the tortured sofa
the sisters sit in state, their
　　　vapid, small faces
　　　　　　contorted
　　　　　　in loathing. Their world
　　　　　　　is this one
　　　　　　lopsided place, this village
carved from stone. Web-footed,
　　　skewered by malice
　　　　　　and chilling winds

   they paper walls
     with the backs of books
as crass as their dreams.

    I think of my dead:
     the wry, sun-burned artist, laughing
as his door slammed shut; of a lover
  slack with cancer,
     refusing my calls
    out of grace. We return
to this: four eyes fixed on
    the cyclops, the sun
  in hiding; the sisters on the sofa,
     snarling at heaven
      from my hell.

WATERLINES

(For Richard Rive, Jack Cope, Steve Bell and Roy Webber)

Life exacts a death
for every year
        on the water's edge. The damp sun
    leaves clean slates
            where their heads
        and gestures
were daubed on our walls.

We home in on the river
to hear its garbled vernacular;
        its phrases of mumbled regret.
    Each year it springs to life, trips
            on its tongue, pronounces
        a death. On the path
    where the water slurs its vowels
    we leave the bones of our shadows,
resurrect; toil on again
        to the source.

All existence flows to that end, it runs
uphill. We pouch our mouths
        at air and words as we salmon
    down to plunge upstream
            through time. Men
    and rivers die; they are eaten
by earth. On the gnawed banks
        a child fumbles at a sextant
    of hands; his small
            paper ship goes out.

In the shallows of our rooms
we fish for words, cast about
        to express our grief. Down the road
    the water garbles

its sermons; the river unfolds
its winding-sheet
over small paper ships
and men.